A Little Goes a Long Way

by Ashley Mills Monaghan
illustrations by Vivian Nguyen

For Liam Finegan and my husband, Dave - your love and support goes a long way. - A.M.M.

To my family and friends, thanks for your endless love and support. - V.N.

Special thanks to Kevin Staniec - a little bit of your guidance went a long way in completing this project.

Stay mindful!

[signature]

2017

Reading Tree Press

Get ideas for your classroom, download the song and audio book,
and read all about the process of making 'A Little Goes a Long Way' at:
www.alittlegoesalongwaybook.com

A Little Goes a Long Way
Written by Ashley Mills Monaghan
Illustrated by Vivian Nguyen
Edited by Kevin Staniec

ISBN - 13: 978-0615927633 (Reading Tree Press)
ISBN - 10: 0615927637

A Little Goes a Long Way

by Ashley Mills Monaghan

illustrations by Vivian Nguyen

This is Fin and his little dog, Sausages.

Fin can be quite messy.

He likes to help with the chores around the house,

but he needs to learn to be more careful.

One day, Fin helped Mom with the dog food.

He scooped
and scooped . . .

and scooped.

Fin helped Dad with the laundry.

He poured

and poured . . .

and poured.

Fin helped Granny cook dinner.

He sprinkled

and sprinkled . . .

and sprinkled.

Fin helped Grandpa in the garden.

He sprayed

and sprayed . . .

and sprayed!

Fin looked around.
He made such a mess.

Just remember, a little goes a long way."

It is a new day.

Fin is helping out again.

Scoop,

scoop . . .

STOP!

Spray,

spray . . .

Everyone was proud of Fin learning to be more careful. They gave him a big kiss and said, "We love you."

Fin didn't know what to say . . .

a little love goes a long way.

The End.

- About the Author -

Ashley Mills Monaghan graduated from Chapman University with a BFA in Film Production and a minor in Music. Originally Ashley pursued a musical career, teaching music in schools and giving private piano lessons. Her first album "Lost and Found" was released in 2007 but she has since pursued other interests. She received her post graduate degree from Saint Nicholas Montessori College Ireland in Early Childhood Education in 2009.
Ashley taught preschool both in Ireland and in the US for several years until she had her first born son, Liam Finegan. She currently resides in Southern California where she enjoys her family, writing stories for children, running, going to the beach and baking.
'A Little Goes a Long Way' is Ashley's first book.

- About the Illustrator -

Vivian Nguyen was born and raised in Arizona - and thanks to the encouragement from family and friends - she knew from an early age that she would want to pursue an artistic career. After graduating from Art Center College of Design in 2002, she spent about eight years in the toy design industry - mostly designing and developing preschool toys and plush for numerous licensed brands. She lives in Los Angeles and currently works as a Flash artist/animator for online games, freelances in illustration and toy design, and participates in various group gallery shows. Her most favorite things in life are family, friends, and ice cream. More of her personal work and sketches can be found at: www.vivdesigns.blogspot.com